Urban Places

Katie Peters

GRL Consultants,
Diane Craig and Monica Marx,
Certified Literacy Specialists

Lerner Publications ◆ Minneapolis

Note from a GRL Consultant
This Pull Ahead leveled book has been carefully designed for beginning readers.
A team of guided reading literacy experts has reviewed and leveled the book to
ensure readers pull ahead and experience success.

Lerner Publications Company
An imprint of Lerner Publishing Group, Inc.
241 First Avenue North
Minneapolis, MN 55401 USA

For reading levels and more information, look up this title at www.lernerbooks.com.

Main body text set in Memphis Pro 24/39
Typeface provided by Linotype.

Photo Acknowledgments
The images in this book are used with the permission of: © Arpad Benedek/iStockphoto,
pp. 12, 13; © f11photo/iStockphoto, pp. 6, 7, 16 (cars); © Harun Ozmen/Shutterstock
Images, pp. 10, 11, 16 (buildings); © Luciano Mortula - LGM/Shutterstock Images,
pp. 4, 5, 16 (signs); © Page Light Studios/iStockphoto, pp. 14, 15; © stu99/iStockphoto,
p. 3; © Victoria Lipov/Shutterstock Images, pp. 8, 9, 16 (windows).

Front cover: © Taiga/Shutterstock

Library of Congress Cataloging-in-Publication Data

Names: Peters, Katie, author.
Title: Urban places / Katie Peters.
Description: Minneapolis : Lerner Publications, 2020. | Series: My community (Pull ahead
    readers—nonfiction) | Includes index. | Audience: Ages 4–7. | Audience: Grades K–1.
    | Summary: "In this nonfiction title, carefully leveled text and full-color photographs
    introduce the emergent reader to all the exciting things to see in a city. Pairs with the
    fiction title Wait, Ride, Walk."— Provided by publisher.
Identifiers: LCCN 2019045816 (print) | LCCN 2019045817 (ebook) | ISBN 9781541590120
    (library binding) | ISBN 9781728403045 (paperback) | ISBN 9781728400600 (ebook)
Subjects: LCSH: Cities and towns—Juvenile literature. | Communities—Juvenile literature.
    | Readers (Primary)
Classification: LCC HT152 .P48 2020 (print) | LCC HT152 (ebook) | DDC 307.76—dc23

LC record available at https://lccn.loc.gov/2019045816
LC ebook record available at https://lccn.loc.gov/2019045817

Manufactured in the United States of America
1 – CG – 7/15/20

Contents

Urban Places

I see many signs.

DO NOT
ENTER

I see many cars.

I see many windows.

I see many buildings.

I see many stores.

I see many people in the city.

Did You See It?

buildings

cars

signs

windows

Index